Celtic Wisdom for Business

Michael Scott

Newleaf

Newleaf

an imprint of
Gill & Macmillan Ltd
Hume Avenue
Park West
Dublin 12
with associated companies throughout the world
www.gillmacmillan.ie

© 2001 Michael Scott
0 7171 3174 2
Print origination by Vermillion
Printed by The Guernsey Press, Guernsey
The paper used in this book is made from the wood
pulp of managed forests. For every tree felled,
at least one tree is planted, thereby reserving
natural resources.

A catalogue record is available for this book from the
British Library.

1 3 5 4 2

There is a magic in words.

A history in them.

Much learning, much knowledge.

Listen to the words and learn from them.

Amergin the Bard

Contents

Introduction

The Celts have been described as warriors and explorers, magicians and artisans, priests and knaves, heroes and kings – but they have always been traders.

Between 700BC and 100AD the Celtic tribes dominated most of Europe. They traded as far south as the African coast, east into the Steppes of Russia, north into the Scandinavian lands, and as far west as the Americas long before Eric the Red or Columbus reached those shores.

Two millennia before the European Economic Union was conceived, a Celtic trade area was effectively in existence, as was a single currency, which was divisible to one twenty-fourth of its value and accepted in markets across Europe.

To facilitate the movement of goods, the Celts cut crude roads through the dense forests which covered most of Europe at the time, paving those roadways with timber and stone. Even the concept of the factory was not unknown to some of the Celtic tribes, and Xenophon (430BC–355BC), the pupil of Socrates, wrote of what can only be described as piece work. 'Here lives the man who cuts shoes, while alongside him lives another who sews them. A simple process, but a successful one.' Throughout the ancient Celtic world, many of the ordinary household utensils look so alike that one is left with the impression that they were mass produced and then traded.

When the Greeks and Romans write of the Celts, it is always to mention their love of luxury and wealth. There is a legion of stories about clever Celts cutting some very good deals – never shady deals, simply good deals, because the Celts treasured reputation and honour. 'Reputation is more enduring than life,' was the great credo of the Celtic Chieftains, and 'Character is better than wealth.'

The Celtic traders learned early on that, 'There is more business to be got with a soft word than on the edge of a sword.' Over time, a loose series of rules was created, some of it advice, more of it just common sense, all of it emphasising honour and fair dealing, and these rules were incorporated into the oral tradition, some finding their way into the Brehon Law which governed all aspects of Celtic life and business.

The honourable deal was everything: both parties had to come away with their pride intact. Concluding a deal was even more important: 'Promising, but not fulfilling, is worse than refusing,' and 'Better not to begin than stop without finishing.'

The Celts, like all the ancient peoples, knew the value of things. Everything they owned, they had either made or traded something they had made for it. We live in a society where people do not know the value of things. The Celts valued items in terms of hard physical labour, skilled craftswork, backbreaking seasons of sowing and tilling, and their own blood and sweat.

That was the cost. 'Everything has a price. Be prepared to pay that price. But be aware that some prices are not worth paying.'

When they traded for the things they could not make themselves, they went shopping with a couple of simple rules:

'Soiled goods are never a bargain.'

'The best bargains are to be got from those in debt.'

'Let the bargain suit the purpose.'

'It is possible to know the price of everything, and to know the value of nothing.'

This collection is drawn from a variety of sources, spans nearly two thousand years, and is as relevant today as it ever was. Many of the phrases and sayings herein are still in use today, not only in the Celtic lands of Ireland, Scotland, Wales, Brittany, Cornwall and the Isle of Man, but across the world, wherever those of Celtic descent have settled. When the Celtic peoples went to the Americas and Canada and Australia, they took with them the sayings of their homelands. In time, these have entered the oral traditions of those countries, and I have endeavoured to include them in this collection. For example,

'Fool me once – shame on you.
Fool me twice – shame on me,'

appears in almost identical form in Ireland, Australia, Canada and parts of America.

The wisdom, proverbs and sayings you will find here are not exclusively for use in business – for the Celts believed that life was business and business was life – and you will find that they will have an application for all aspects of life.

Business is Life …

There are three people one should
never do business with:
The person too eager,
The person too greedy, and
The person too desperate.

There are three people the businessman
should never deal with:
The liar
The thief and
The knave,
For to deal with them is to become
like them.

Watch the hen; its feathers remain
ruffled until its brood is reared.

If you must be in rags, then let your rags
be tidy.

Let your clothes be respectful – to
yourself and your client.

Allow the clothes to suit the purpose.

There is a time for everything; only the
fool goes out to thresh on a windy day.

There is much to be heard from a
closed mouth.

Beware the man who is too open with his favours and his friendship, for one day he will look for payment.

Watch for the man who gives too freely of his friendship and advice, for they are often worthless.

A contract can be cancelled up to the time the sun sets on the day that it is made, but once the sun has set, the contract is irrevocable.

Remember this: you live in the shadow of your neighbour.

Never forget that you stand on the shoulders of your staff.

Everything has a price, but there are some prices that are not worth paying.

Speak about your customers as if they were your family. And treat them accordingly.

Cheat your partner – and you cheat yourself.

Walk slowly on the new path.

A craft badly learned is a craft destroyed.

Work not in a job:
which you do not enjoy,
which does not pay you well, and
which treats you ill.

Plan for the tomorrow that will never come.

Be careful and these three will be yours:
Respect,
Abundance, and
Contentment.

Be always timid and you will achieve,
Nothing good,
Nothing bad,
Nothing.

Even stone will crack if the fire is hot
enough.

It is easier to scatter than it is to gather.
But it is only possible to gather when
one has sown.

If you wait for the fine day to do
business, you will wait forever.

The tree remains, but not the hand that
planted it.

The cow that's first up gets the best of
the morning's dew.

Praise the fine day in the evening.

These are the three aspirations
of the honest man:
To be honest in one's dealings
with others,
To be honest in one's dealing
with one's partner, and
To be honest in one's dealing
with oneself.

And there are three further aspirations
of the honest man:
To conduct oneself with dignity
and pride,
To conduct one's business with dignity
and pride, and
To conclude one's business with oneself
and others with dignity and pride.

Success is dependent upon three things:
Wisdom,
Consideration, and
Expertise.

Success stems from action and there are
three ways to act:
By thought,
By word, and
By deed.

There are only three habits that lead to
success:
Patience,
Application, and
Vision.

There are always three habits that lead
to failure:
Laziness,
Distraction, and
Daydreaming.

There is a time for dreaming, and a
time for doing.
It is the wise man who knows the
difference.

When only one song is heard,
only one melody can be heard.

Good business is like a bagpipe – you have to fill it to make it work.

It is the work which praises the man. Take pride in the work.

Some of the sweetest berries grow among the sharpest thorns.
But these are the only berries worth striving for.

Time drags for the waiting man, flies for the rushing man,
And time will not be hurried.

The greatest pleasure in life lies in doing
that which people say we cannot do.

There are three ways to ensure
excellence in all things:
To be moderate in thought and
behaviour,
To hold to one's oaths, and
To accept one's responsibilities.

Do not gut your fish till you have
landed them.

When a log burns at both ends it will
last but a short time,
But it will give off just as much heat as
if it burned at one end.

When the sun shines is the time to
make up hay.

He who will not prosper in his sleep
will not prosper when awake.

The lion is known by the scratch
of his claw.

There is always only one call to meat,
And always two to work.

What goes far from the eye, will
eventually go far from the heart.

Success is always deserved.

The idle hand gets nothing.

Idleness deserves nothing.

Lie down with dogs and you will rise up with fleas.

Better not to begin than stop without finishing.

He who would enjoy the fruit must not spoil the blossom.

There are three who will always work with a hump:
The writer,
The tailor, and
The cat.

A good tale is not the worse of being twice told.

The best business is conducted in good weather.

Even the truth sounds foolish when shouted aloud and laughter will make a lie of any truth.

The best business is conducted in whispers.

Ne'er do business with a man who is loud for he will shout your secrets as easily as he shouts his own.

A long thread suggests a lazy tailor, a roughened plank a lazy carpenter. The work proclaims the man. Be proud of your work.

A little dog can startle a hare, but it takes a big one to catch it. Make sure that you are that big dog.

It is the foolish dog that shows his teeth too early. The wise dog will only show his teeth when he is ready to bite.

A good deal is good business, but a bad deal is a mistake.

There is truth in wine; listen to the wine drinker.

Remember that bees with honey in their mouths have stings in their tails.

Do not complain about good fortune.
Do not complain about ill luck.
They are two sides of the one coin.
Simply turn the coin over.

In business one needs only the gifts of
the fox: a good eye and a sharp ear, and
the ability to pounce.

Is it better to know everything,
Or to know everyone?

Take care to look after your own
business, lest someone else do it
for you.

The load is made up of small handfuls.

If we forget what has gone before, how
can we plan for the future?

The future is born out of the present,
which has its seeds in the past.
A seed, carefully planted in the past,
nurtured in the present,
will yield a bounty in the future.

A field is never ploughed by turning it over in the mind.

One cannot be numbered amongst the flock, but bleat like a goat.

No door closes without another opening.

Some doors should never be opened; others should be quickly shut.
Know the difference; know when to open and when to shut those doors.

Do the deed right first time, for there
will be many who will attempt to undo
it afterwards.

There is a lot of big talk from little
work.

One will never tire of a profitable
occupation.

Discipline brings its own luck.

Begin the job,
Then, finish it.

A tame gosling was never reared by a
wild goose.
Remember who you are dealing with,
no matter what face is presented.

Beware the business founded by the
father and now run by the son.
Do not confuse them for they are
different beasts indeed.

Deal with the dog – and not with the pup.

The dog barks,
The pup whimpers.

It is no secret when three know it.
It is no secret when it has been shared.

See that your own hearth is swept
before you lift your neighbour's ashes.

Great gaps may be filled with small
stones.

Follow your feet, for they will always
take you to your heart's desire.
Have the courage to follow your feet.

A man with good boots does not mind
where he places his foot.

Even the longest road has a turning.

The fool desires only idleness.
And the fool gets what he deserves.

It is the wisest fisherman who listens to
the sound of the river
before he casts his line.

The fish is not caught 'till it is landed,
cooked and eaten.

Do not judge by appearances; a rich
heart may be under a poor coat.

Listen, but not with your ears,
Watch, but not with your eyes,
Speak, but not with your mouth.

There are three roads to greatness:
To be wise in word,
To be wise in deed, and
To be wise enough to control one's own
passions.

Let All Your Dealings
be Honourable ...

There are three things that are better
than riches:
Health,
Freedom, and
Honour.
For when all else has passed, only
honour remains.
And this all men remember.

There are three things from which one
should never stray:
Belief in oneself,
Belief in a higher self, and
Belief in the truth.

Better one good thing that is now,
Than two things that were once.

True greatness knows gentleness.
True gentleness can achieve greatness.
Strive for greatness.

Those who perpetuate injustice share
three common traits:
They are arrogant,
They are liars, and
They are cowards,
And ultimately, they are doomed to
ignominy and failure.

Pride can strip us of these three things:
Time,
Money, and
Conscience.
Pride can bring a great man down,
and it can raise the lowliest to a great
height.

A big belly, an ungenerous heart.
An ungenerous heart, a bitter soul.
A bitter soul, a troubled past.
A troubled past, an uncertain future.

Patience cures all ills, but how many
have the patience to allow the ill to be
cured?

Every person of business should defend their staff, for it is the staff who bring the profits. Honour them, and they, in turn, will honour you.

A kind heart is better than a crafty head. And will achieve more.

A man should be prepared to die to save his honour. For what else is there?

No-one is safe from a liar. Shun them, for the man that lies for you today, will lie to you tomorrow.

Be seen in the company of a known liar
and a rogue, and you will be counted
as one.

Honourable company brings honour.
Disreputable company brings its own
reputation.

It is difficult to soothe the proud, for
their pride blinds them.

A wise man often conciliates his
enemy; the fool will only aggrieve him.

To be and having been are not the same.

It is better to be, than to have once been.

A gossip's mouth is the devil's postbag. Listen not to it, and take care never to feed it.

Take not your advice from the loser.

When all else has passed, only truth
and honour remain.

All tides will eventually ebb ...
excepting the tide of graciousness.

Often the bitter cup we strive to remove
from us holds the medicine we are most
in need of. Remember, the truth is
often close at hand, but unpalatable.

Even the smallest bird is a heavy
burden when carried far.
Share the burden and it will be
lightened.

It is only the wearer who knows where
the shoe pinches.

Better to know than to be told.
Better to learn than to acquire.

To achieve what others have achieved,
all one has to do is to work for it.

Is it honest to steal from a thief?

You cannot do good to other people
without doing good to yourself.

Evil thoughts often come from
idleness.
Idleness leads to ruin.

It is easier to get into trouble than
to get out.

Waste neither time nor advice
on the fool.
They will not listen,
They will not heed,
And they do not care.

Justice wrongs no man.

Beware secrets. A secret is a weapon. It
can be used either by you ... or against
you.

A still tongue is better than bitter
speaking.

Bitter talk often bites the talker.

It is good to be knowledgeable, but
better to be lovable.
The loved will never want for
companionship.

Never seek the fight,
But never shun it either.
There is only one victor in a battle,
And that is victory.

Choose him for a friend who incites
you to good works.

Take pride in the company of
honourable men.

There is no honour in anger; whatever
the outcome, restrain your emotions.

There is no shame in speaking the
truth.

He who is guilty himself, will always be
urging others to injustice.

He who tells you the faults of others
will tell your faults to them.

He who seeks for a friend without a
fault will never find him. But friends
are blind to the faults of their
companions.

It is better to be remembered in the
prayers of a good man than in the will
of a rich man. For one will surely bring
its eventual reward, while the other
might bring only tears.

A man never thinks of the evil he did
not do.

Good deeds are never regretted,
Evil deeds are never forgotten.

There is no shame in error:
The first error is overlooked,
The second error is noted,
And the third is acted upon.

A known liar will never be believed
even though he speaks the truth. Take
care never to be known as a liar, for it is
something which will follow you to
your grave.

A man is known by his company.

He who gets imposed upon is mocked.
He who allows himself to be imposed
upon is a fool.

To every cow its calf.
To every book its copy.
To every workman his share.

A fool will not receive praise, and a wise
man will not receive rebuke.

Reputation is more enduring than life.

Character is better than wealth.

The man who will acknowledge no
judge condemns himself.

Falling is easier than rising.
But having fallen many times, it is
easier to rise.

Anger may visit the heart of a wise
man,
But it abides always in the heart of the
foolish, the greedy and the envious.
And where there is anger, there is little
room for any other emotion.

If it is worth taking, it is worth
asking for.
And if it is worth asking for,
It is worth working for.

A man's faults will grow as large as a
mountain ere he himself sees them,
though he can see the tiniest speck of
his companion's fault.

Better than gold is the tale well told,
and more valuable.

It is truly said that treachery always
returns to its source.

It is better to be content with the small portion that comes with a blessing than the large portion that comes with a curse.

When the deal is done and the price is paid, all that remains is honour.

The rogue is often well-dressed and well-spoken. Look beyond the clothes and the words to find the real man.

An empty house is preferable to a bad tenant.

The truth is sometimes bitter to swallow.
But like all good medicine, it must be taken.

Money and Debt, Oft' Two Sides of the Same Coin ...

How many know the price of a thing,
but not its value!
And there are some things which have
no price and are beyond value.

Beware the man who knows how many
grains there are in a bushel of wheat
and who has never tasted bread.

The weak are vulnerable to the lure
of money.
And weakness has little to do with
wealth.

Forgetting a debt does not pay it.
Remembering the debt ensures it is
honoured.

A promise is a debt.
Honour your promises and your debts.

Choice is a luxury,
But the poor cannot even afford that.

When something is got badly, it'll be
sure to go badly.

Pay a little, get a little,
Pay a little more, get a lot more.

How many mourn the want
of possessions!
Yet the strong, the brave, and the rich,
all go to the grave at last,
Like the poor, the emaciated,
and the infant.
And none take their possessions with them.

It is sad to have no friend,
Sad to have unfortunate children;
Sad to have only a poor hut;
But it is sadder still to have nothing at
all – be it good or bad.

Money has a short tail,
And cannot be easily held.

Better an old debt than an old grudge,
But sometimes an old debt begets an old
grudge,
And an old grudge never ages.

Borrow neither from a neighbour
Nor a friend.
And you will keep both.

Many a defect is seen in the poor man when,
in reality, the only defect is the poverty.

Give freely without the expectation of a
return,
Then you will never be disappointed,
But you will often be surprised.

Time diminishes all things – except greed.

The father is responsible for the child
and the debts of the child.
A child remains a child until he is ten
and seven years.

If a child is given everything, then the
child will grow to maturity knowing
the value of nothing.
But if the child is given nothing, then
he too will grow to maturity knowing
the value of nothing. Give something.

Give a little to those with nothing.
It will seem a lot,
Though it will still be a little to you.

It is truly said that possession satisfies.
It simply never satisfies enough.

A heavy purse makes for a heavy heart,
Though a light purse makes for an
equally heavy heart.

There is many a gift given that's
eventually paid for.
Take a care what gifts you accept.

Pay staff and keep staff.

Remember this: everything fades, but
some things fade faster than others.

Like a big voice from a big ram, but
with very little wool on it. Ignore it.

Loud talk, little ideas.

Man does not need for much:
A clean shirt,
A little money in the pocket
And a clear conscience are enough.

There is no poverty in good land.

Beware the man who offers you his
ideas without charge, for they are
worth as much.
Beware the man who will charge you
for developing your ideas, for he has
none of his own.

Without money fame is dead.

The rich can afford compassion;
the poor give of it freely.

A full stomach cannot understand the
empty stomach.

Good fortune often abides with a fool,
but it is still good fortune.

A fool and a fortune are often quickly
separated.

What is delayed will be often forgotten
– but only by one of the parties, and
never by both.

It is not the man who has little that
is poor,
It is the man who has it all, yet pines
after even more.

One can have some money and be happy,
But one cannot have no money and be
happy.

The man who tells you that one can be
poor and happy, is a liar.

Better to be poor and honest
Than to be rich and lying,
And it is better to be born lucky,
than rich.

Foolish spending is the father
of poverty.

The remembrance of the heart is
more valuable than the remembrance
of the head.

One who lets by; one who puts off.

Credit will come to payment.
Credit shall reach the door.

The longer the credit term, the shorter
the memory.

Long credit devalues the goods.

Eaten bread is quickly forgotten.

The full belly never feels for the hunger.
The empty belly is always wanting.

Promising but not fulfilling is worse
than refusing.

Be generous to others and they, in turn,
will be generous to you.

Generosity should come from the heart, not from the head.

What may be done at any time will be done at no time.

Pity the man who loves only coin, for he is poor indeed.

A little, often, leaves wrinkles in the fabric of a purse.

There is honour in having lived well,
There is honour in having fought well,
There is honour in dying well,
But there is no honour in poverty.

A bad bird will lay a bad egg.

The beggar will not be troubled by
a thief.

There are three things that make a fool
wise:
Learning,
Application, and
Patience.

And there are three things that make
a wise man foolish:
Quarrelling,
Rage, and
Drunkenness.

There are three paths to downfall:
To allow one's passions to rule,
To be self-indulgent, and
To refuse to learn by the example
of others.

Personal experience is always valuable
experience.

May there always be work for you to do,
And then work like you don't need
to work.

Money brings friends, but not the
friends you want it to bring.

Beware the friend you can buy.

A full purse brings many friends, and
all of them worthless.

A little pleases a poor man whereas
even a lot never pleases the rich man.

Common Sense is
Far from Common ...

There is more business to be done with
a soft word than on the edge of a sword.

There are three things which all men
seek more of:
A long and happy life,
Unfailing good health, and
Abundant wealth.

There are three things which all men
seek less of:
Sickness,
Poverty, and
Loneliness.

It is truly said that he who is late rising will be in a hurry all day.

There is no fireside like your own fireside.

If something needs to be done, it will be done, but first one must have the desire to do it. Otherwise, there will only be excuses.

The greatest gift that God can give us is to see ourselves as others see us.

It is not only the cow that is milked
from her head.

There is no shame in not knowing;
There is shame, however, in not
learning.

Forgive the mistake, but do not forget it.

Only the fool will not learn from his
error, and his crime is to repeat it
endlessly.

Instinct is stronger than upbringing.

When the drink is inside good sense is outside.

Time passes, death strikes.
And sometimes one is slow and the other swift, but no-one knows which.

In times of necessity no law is recognised.

The one who sulks with his food
surprises his rear-end.

For being wrinkled, a good apple has
not lost its flavour.

The horse which resists his rider's spurs
will do his sides a great injustice.

One time gives birth to another.

Strive for boldness in all things.
Therein lies the route to success in all
things.

He who holds his tongue keeps his
friend.

It is better to fight with a friend than to
fight with an enemy.

Beware your tongue – it will cut your
throat.

Many a deal foundered with a flapping tongue.

It is better to ask, and sound foolish for an instant,
Than never to ask, and remain foolish forever.

Feckless fools should keep canny tongues.

Beware of what you say, for you may hear it again.

Think more than you say.
Say less than you mean.

His head will never fill his father's
bonnet.

Wishing and dreaming,
Oft confused
But they are not the same, and it is the
wise man who knows the difference.

It is not the cow that shouts most
which milks the best.
But the cow that shouts most is
milked first.

It is better to have a mouth of ivy and
a heart of holly.

Envy and anger do little but shorten
one's life.

A shared joy is doubled,
A shared sorrow is halved.

Self praise travels no distance.

Listen to the speaker, not the words.

A wet Christmas, a fat churchyard.

A friend by thy side is better than a brother far off.

Let your anger set with the sun, and then ensure that it does not rise again the following morn with it.

A friend is someone who will sit by
your side, and not in your place.

The truth is sometimes bitter; do not
dismiss the unpalatable truth.

Think before you speak,
Think before you act,
And then think again.

More men are lost by being too wise
than by being too unwise.

There is no disease more dangerous
than to be without knowledge.
It is not coin which revolves the world;
it is knowledge.
It will come to us if we will wait
long enough.
And provided we place ourselves
in the right location.

Never be ashamed to confess
your faults.
But first, recognise those faults.

The coroner and the lawyer grow fat
on the quarrels of fools.

A wise man can form a year's
judgement from a single night's
knowledge of another man.

A big head on a wise man and a hen's
head on a fool.

Empty vessels make the most noise,
and it sounds like the laughter of
drunken fools.

The hasty man is seldom out of trouble.

The deepest streams flow with the
least noise.

A great head with little wit, and a little
head without any.

Between two stools is a fall.

A day's work – getting started.
A day's work – never done.

Never lift the younger up until he has
fallen, for it is only by falling that he
learns.

The more haste the more hindrance.

Every day has its night, every weal
its woe.

The thing that is scarce is the most
wonderful.
And things can be made scarce.

One look before is better than two
behind.

It is better to measure twice, so that you
can cut only once.
It is better to strike small and often,
than once and badly.

The man that opens his mouth the
most, opens his heart the least.

It is far better to be alone than in bad
company.

The company of thieves, knaves and
fools is no company.

There is little point in buying bread
from a butcher, or meat from a baker.
To each his own craft.

Many a ship has sunk within the
harbour walls.

Cleverness is better than strength.

The tongue ties knots stronger than any rope.

The willing horse is often overburdened.
There are times when it is better not to be the willing horse.

Don't go for the doctor when the patient is dead.

Never dance in a small boat.

Idleness is a fool's desire.

Even the wise man has his faults.
And he knows them.
The fool does not recognise his faults.

The fool wanders, the wise one travels.

Understanding comes later.

Say but little and say it well.

He who will not look before him, will look behind him.

Timely advice is better than a late gift.

Have a name for knowing more than you know,
And you will be asked little.
Have a name for rising early,
And you may stay abed till noon.

Advice is wasted on the foolish, the
arrogant and the greedy.

A small spark has often kindled
a great fire.

Do not light a fire that you cannot
yourself put out.

Choose your company before you
choose your drink.

The world will pass away, but love and music will endure.

There are three that come unsought, unbidden and often undesired:
Fear,
Jealousy, and
Love.

Remember there are two tellings to every story. Make sure you listen to both sides.

When there is no cure, there is
patience.
With patience comes understanding.
With understanding comes knowledge.
With knowledge comes power.

Acknowledgements

A book of this nature grows out of many sources. It is, effectively, the sum of more than twenty years research into Celtic folklore.

In those years many people have given freely of their time and allowed me access to their libraries and I would like to acknowledge their help and kindness.

However, no book would ever come to publication without the enthusiasm and encouragement of a publisher and, in this case,

I was well served by Gill & Macmillan. I would like to acknowledge both Michael Gill and Peter Thew who enthused and encouraged in equal measure.